by
Émilie BEAUMONT

Illustrated by
Lindsey SELLEY

· DISCOVERING ANIMALS ·

FARM ANIMALS

by
Émilie Beaumont

Illustrated by
Lindsey Selley

TRODDY
BOOKS

Cattle

Female cattle are called cows. The male is called a bull, and the young are called calves. Bulls are bigger than cows.

The cow produces milk for her calf, and also for us. The milk comes from udders under her stomach. Cows spend most of their time in the fields eating grass. The farmer brings them in to milk them twice a day. In winter, when the weather is bad, they live in a cow shed, and the farmer gives them hay to eat.

The sound that cows make is called 'mooing', or lowing.

Chewing the cud

When cows graze, they swallow the grass quickly. Later, they bring it up into their mouths again and chew it for a long time. This is called chewing the cud. The cows munch the grass into a pulp before swallowing it again. Chewing the cud makes the grass easier to digest.

A bull, a cow and her calf.

Bulls can be dangerous. Don't go into a field where there is a bull.

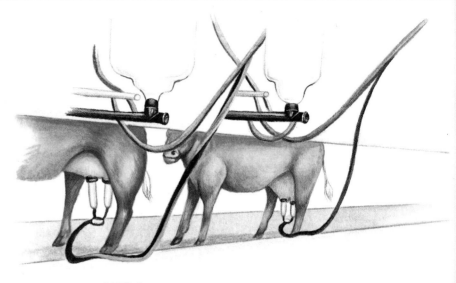

Milking

Once, cows were milked by hand. That was often the job of the farmer's wife. Milking took a long time, and it was not easy. The farmer's wife might get a kick from a hoof, or a swish from a tail. These days, farmers have machines to do the milking.

Different kinds of cows

There are many different kinds of cows. You can tell which breed they are by their colour. Some are brown or black, and some have big white patches. Some breeds of cow give more milk than others. Some give creamier milk.

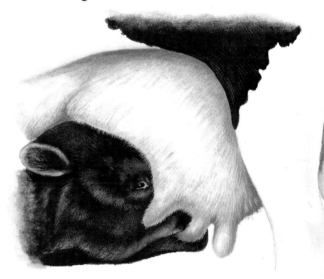

Hungry calves

As soon as it is born, the little calf begins to feed. It takes milk from its mother several times a day, until it is old enough to eat grass.

Pigs

Pigs always seem to be hungry, and they are not very fussy about what they eat. You can recognise a pig by its fat body, and by its big snout and its little curly tail.

Pigs eat potatoes, apples and carrots, as well as meat scraps and special pig food, which is made in a factory. People think pigs are dirty, but really they are clean animals. A pig may roll in the mud, but not because it likes getting muddy. The mud protects its skin from the sun.

Pigs have large families

The mother pig, or sow, has many piglets at the same time. When she lies down with her baby piglets, she has to be watched carefully. Because she is so fat she may crush them without noticing. The piglets grow very fast. When they are six months old, they weigh 100 kg.

Different kinds of pigs

You can tell what breed a pig belongs to by looking at the shape of its snout and ears. Some have long snouts, or long ears, some have short ones. Some have ears which stand up straight, and some have floppy ears that fall over their eyes. Some breeds are not pink, but black or black and white. Some are spotted.

Hunting for truffles

Pigs have a very good sense of smell. In some places they are used to find truffles, which are like mushrooms but grow underground. People, as well as pigs, enjoy truffles. Pigs find them by smell, and dig them out with their snouts.

Muddy pigs

Pigs do not like too much heat or sunlight. If there is no water nearby, they wallow in mud to cool themselves.

The mother pig is called a sow, the babies are piglets, and the father is a hog.

Pigs make a grunting noise, which sounds like 'oink-oink'.

Horses

The horse is a beautiful animal. With its long legs, it can run very fast, and it is the most intelligent of farm animals. Horses have been the servants of men and women for thousands of years. They were the main form of transport before railways and motor cars. They pulled carts and carriages on the roads and drew ploughs on the farms. Today, horses have gone from streets and farms, but they still give us sport and entertainment. People everywhere enjoy horse-racing, circus riding and show-jumping. Pony riding is popular in the country and in city parks.

The foal

The foal takes milk from its mother for about six months. By that time, it has also learned to eat grass in the pasture. It stays close to its mother and likes to play and run beside her.

Feeding horses

In pastures or fields, horses eat the grass. When the weather is cold, they live in a stable, and eat oats and hay, or straw.

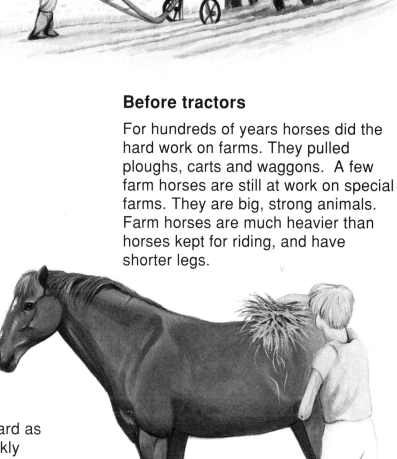

Before tractors

For hundreds of years horses did the hard work on farms. They pulled ploughs, carts and waggons. A few farm horses are still at work on special farms. They are big, strong animals. Farm horses are much heavier than horses kept for riding, and have shorter legs.

Farm horses

Although horses do not often work on farms now, you can still see many horses in the countryside. Most of them are kept for riding, or are trained as race-horses.

The hooves of a horse are not as hard as they look. They are worn down quickly and can be damaged by hard ground. They must be protected with metal horse-shoes. Blacksmiths make the horse-shoes and fit them to the horse's hooves.

Looking after a horse

Horses sleep in stables. They need lots of clean, dry straw in their stalls. After riding, they are rubbed down well, and their coats are brushed to keep them shining.

The noise that horses make is called neighing or whinnying.

Sheep

The first sheep came from dry countries, but some of today's breeds like a different climate. They enjoy wetter countries, where the grass is greener. Farmers raise sheep mainly for wool and for meat. In some places sheep are kept also for their milk, which is made into cheese. The female sheep, called a ewe, has one or two lambs, which are born in the spring. The lambs feed on the ewe's milk for four or five months. When they are a few weeks old, their tails are docked, or cut short. Otherwise the tails would grow very long and get dirty.

A shepherd's life

The shepherd watches over his flock of sheep. He is often helped by his dog,

Ram

Lamb

Different kinds of sheep

Some breeds of sheep have curling horns. Others have no horns. Some have pricked-up ears, others have floppy ears. Some have a very thick coat, called a fleece. Some breeds have short legs, others long legs.

which rounds up sheep that stray. The shepherd looks after sick animals, and he helps the ewes at lambing time.

Shearing

To make the best wool, the sheep's fleece is removed in one piece. Sheep-shearers used to do this with clippers, but today they have electric shears. Sheep are shorn in the spring, when the weather is getting warmer, so they will not catch cold. They are happier without a thick fleece in the summer. The fleece of the sheep is made into fine wool, and the wool is made into clothes. Your best jumper came from sheep.

Sheep make a bleating noise, which sounds like 'Ba-a-a'.

Ewe

Goats

Goats are tough animals. They can live in all kinds of country, even on stony mountains. They do not mind wet or cold weather, and they eat almost anything that grows. They like grass best, but they also eat branches and leaves of trees.

The female goat is called a nanny goat. The male is a billy goat, and a young goat is called a kid. Goats are kept for their milk, which is made into tasty cheese.

Goats make a bleating noise, like sheep.

Different kinds of goats

There are many different kinds of goats. Many have horns. Some have long, floppy ears, others have short, pricked-up ears. Their coats may be long and woolly, but most farm goats have short hair.

Out in the pasture

Goats can be kept on high mountains. They like open spaces, and they climb about in dangerous places without slipping or falling. The goatherd, with his dog, keeps an eye on them.

Goats that stray

Goats are explorers. They will wander far away to look for food, if they can. To stop them eating crops, they must be kept in a field with fences. Sometimes, they are tied to a stake on a long rope.

Kids

Kids are usually born in the spring. Some nanny goats have two or even three kids at once. The kids feed on their mother's milk when they are very young. After a few weeks, they learn to graze on grass.

15

Ducks

Like all farm animals, ducks were once wild creatures. Farm ducks were bred from wild ones thousands of years ago. They are fatter than their wild cousins, and they hardly fly at all, although wild ducks fly very high and fast. But farm ducks, like wild ones, must have some water to swim in. A farm that has ducks also has a duckpond.

Ducks are raised for eating, but some people like to eat ducks' eggs too.

Male ducks are called drakes, and the young ones are ducklings. When they are hatched, ducklings are like fluffy balls with a beak and two little eyes. They do not follow their mother into the duckpond until they are about four weeks old.

Ducks that live near a pond must be carefully watched. They are not very careful where they lay their eggs, and sometimes the eggs fall into the water.

Help from a hen

Before she lays her eggs, the duck builds a cosy nest of feathers. She often makes her nest out of sight in a far corner of the farmyard. Sometimes, the farmer gets a hen to sit on the duck's eggs in a place where he can keep an eye on them. The duck does not seem to mind.

Breeds of ducks

Most farm ducks have white feathers, but some breeds are different colours. The white Aylesbury duck, which is named after an English town, is often raised for eating.

Hungry ducks

Ducks are easy to feed. The farmer gives them bread and grain, but they like to find other food themselves. They enjoy a juicy worm, or fresh green leaves. They even eat stinging nettles, if the nettles are chopped up.

The duck's call is a loud *'Quack-quack'*.

Chickens

The female chicken is called a hen and the male a cock. The babies are called chicks. The cock is larger, stronger and more handsome than the hen. He looks very proud of himself as he struts about. If two cocks are kept together, they may fight to decide who is king of the farmyard. When that happens, they must be separated. When the sun rises at the beginning of the day, the cock begins his loud crowing. He is a very good alarm clock. Hens do not crow. They make a soft clucking sound. They often cluck when they have just laid an egg, as if they are pleased with themselves.

Weasel

Fox

Polecat

The chicken's enemies

Chickens must be kept in a safe hen house. They have enemies outside, such as foxes and weasels. These hunters lurk near the hen house, hoping to find a way to break in.

Laying eggs

The farmer wants his hens to lay their eggs in the right place. So he makes up a nice nest of straw and puts a china egg in it. If he is lucky, the hen will lay her own eggs there. Eggs must be collected every day. An egg that is found outside the nest is not safe to eat.

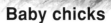

Baby chicks

The hen's nest is put somewhere where she will not be disturbed. Once a day, she leaves the nest to feed. That gives the farmer a chance to look at the nest and make sure the eggs are all right. He takes out any cracked or broken ones. The hen sits on her eggs for about 21 days, until they hatch. At first the little chicks are fluffy and yellow. When they are older, they grow feathers like their parents.

Hens fight too

Life in the hen house is not always peaceful. Not only cocks get into fights. Some hens are bad-tempered too. They will peck at hens weaker than they are, to show who is the boss.

Feeding chickens

Chickens eat corn and grain, which the farmer gives them. They also scratch about for worms in the farmyard, and pick at grass and other green plants.

Rabbits

Rabbits are often kept as pets, as well as for fur and meat. They have babies several times in one year, with six to ten babies in each litter.

Rabbits eat all kinds of green plants, like clover, dandelions and grass. Never give them wet grass, because it will make them ill. They also eat vegetable scraps, as well as oats, barley, and special food sold in pet shops. Rabbits that eat a lot of greens do not drink very much. But rabbits do need water.

Rabbits in a run

Rabbits can live in the open, in a field or garden. The field must have a wire fence to stop them escaping. The fence also keeps out hungry foxes.

Breeds of rabbits

There are many breeds of rabbits, with different coats and different sizes. Some breeds, like the Angora (above left), have long, silky coats. Most breeds have short coats. You can tell the breed by its colour or its markings. Dutch rabbits (above centre) are white at the front and black or coloured at the back.

Young rabbits

When baby rabbits are born, they are blind and have no fur. They grow up fast, and in eight or nine days they are covered with soft fur. After about 15 days they open their eyes and start to move about the hutch.

Rabbit hutches

Rabbits live in cages called hutches. The males, called bucks, are kept separate from the does, or females. Bucks also need separate hutches, or they may fight each other. Rabbits hate being wet or dirty, so the hutches must be cleaned often.

Turkeys

Turkeys first came from America, but now they are raised in many parts of the world. They are raised for their meat. At Christmas time, many families have turkey for dinner.

The turkey is the largest bird in the farmyard. It is over one metre long and weighs 15 or 16 kg. Turkeys need plenty of space to wander about and peck at grass and weeds in the farmyard. They are funny-looking birds, fat with a tail shaped like a fan. Bags of loose red skin hang from the sides of their heads.

A busy mother

The hen turkey lays her eggs in spring. Sometimes she lays more in autumn. She looks for a quiet corner, away from other farmyard fowls. The farmer must keep an eye on the turkey chicks when they are hatched, as the heavy mother bird can crush them by mistake. Because turkeys hate the cold and wet, they are often raised indoors.

Quarrelsome turkeys

The turkey is a strong, powerful bird. It will bully the smaller farmyard fowls, such as ducks and hens.

Although turkeys have red heads, they do not like to see the colour red. If a turkey sees a girl wearing a bright red dress, it grows angry and nervous.

Different kinds of turkeys

Some turkeys are all white or all black. Others are dark with shiny green or reddish tints in their feathers. They are not beautiful birds, but a turkey with its tail feathers spread out like a fan is a fine sight.

Turkeys make a a gobbling noise.

Geese

Geese look like big ducks, with very long necks, short legs and strong wings.

Farmers keep geese for their feathers, as well as for meat.

Geese also act as guards of the farmyard. If a stranger, or a fox, comes into the yard, the cackling of the geese sounds an alarm.

The male is called a gander. It is larger than the female goose. The young birds are called goslings.

Geese like to eat grains such as oats and corn. They also like to peck at leafy plants.

Careless mothers

In February or March, when geese are getting ready to lay their eggs, the farmer watches them carefully. The mother goose will often hide her eggs somewhere, to keep them safe. While she is sitting on them, she sometimes forgets to eat. The farmer must make sure she is fed. But when the goslings are hatched, the mother soon forgets about them. Sometimes she goes away and leaves them before they are all hatched.

Unfriendly geese

Ganders have bad tempers. They may fight each other, and they may attack other animals, including people! Do not try to pet a goose unless you know it well. You may get a nasty surprise.

Goslings hate water

Young goslings have soft, downy feathers. The rain quickly soaks them, and they may catch cold and even die. They like plenty of water to drink, but they don't like it on their feathers.

Geese make a loud honking or cackling noise. If they are angry, they may hiss like a snake.

Guinea fowl

These handsome birds are related to chickens and turkeys, but they are not so common.

They are grey in colour, or a mixture of black and white. The female, or hen, is about the same size as a small chicken. On her head she has a little red crest, but no feathers.

Guinea fowl like to live in groups. You do not often see one on its own.

The cocks can be bad-tempered. They like to chase chickens and other farmyard fowls.

Sticking together

Guinea fowl like to stay together in groups. Chickens will go exploring on their own, but not guinea fowl. When they do wander off with the chickens, they stay with the group and return to the farmyard together.

A big happy family

Young guinea fowl are better behaved than their fathers. They are often raised with chickens, and get on very well with them. Chickens and guinea fowl have the same habits. They wander about pecking at grain or seeds and digging up worms and ant's eggs.

Hiding the eggs

The guinea fowl hides its eggs in strange places, such as bushes or dead tree trunks. The chicks start to run about as soon as they are hatched.

Guinea fowl are not noisy birds. They sometimes make a whining noise, as if they are complaining about something.

CONTENTS

Typeset by TPS Ltd, London

This edition published in 1992 by
Regency House Publishing Limited
The Grange
Grange Yard
London
SE1 3AG

Printed in Italy
ISBN 1 85361 301 0